SUGGESTIONS & SOLUTIONS: EVERYDAY OBSERVATIONS BLOG

The purpose of this blog is to **enlighten** my readers of what is really going on, on the news front.

To find solutions or be an advocate for certain causes. And, also to **bring about awareness** of certain issues to our communities.

Advocate for:

- Against Violence

- Against Animal Cruelty

- Pro-Uber

- Meetup.com

- Createspace.com

- Shark Tank

tRNS - transcranial random noise stimulation

(http://io9.gizmodo.com/new-brain-stimulation-technique-makes-you-better-at-mat-506925851)

"it works by enhancing the excitability of the brain, and it does so by applying random electrical noise to target regions of the cortex via stimulation electrodes placed on the surface of the scalp...non=invasive, painless and cheap"

"It could also help people with learning disabilities or neurodegenerative disorders like Alzheimer's or Parkinson's."

Only issue is that it is relatively new. So the long-term effects are unknown.

Entirely different topic: **Feminine Care**

(http://www.redtentwellness.com)

"The vaginal steam bath is actually eons old and is seen in almost every indigenous culture and many mostly Eastern cultures as a common and routine ritual for women's health. It is commonly used in almost all of the Caribbean, Mexico, Belize and Guatemala and in each region of the globe the native plants and flowers are used for their soothing, energizing and even antiviral/antibacterial properties."

Very good to know: **Liability Insurance**

(https://www.nationwide.com/small-business-liability-insurance.jsp)

"With the day-to-day uncertainties of business management, liability insurance is something you cannot do without. Accidents happen – on site, off site, with employees and with customers – no matter how much you've planned. It is a critical part of any insurance portfolio, regardless of your industry.

Liability insurance can help cover medical expenses, attorney fees and damages you are legally responsible for. It can also offer protection against situations that may not have even crossed your mind. For example, any individual or business providing an opinion, making recommendations, designing products/solutions or offering a service is at risk for a professional liability lawsuit. Nationwide can help with defense costs, regardless of fault, as well as protection for judgments, court costs and more."

Emotional Therapy Dog vs. Service Animal Factoids

(https://www.esaregistration.org/faq/)

"An **emotional support animal** is just that. It's a dog that belongs to somebody who has emotional needs. Sometimes people will refer to them as "therapy dogs" or "comfort dogs" but this is not recognized by the Americans with Disabilities Act.

The person must have a mental health professional determine that the presence of a dog is necessary for them to continue their daily living habits. They are also **required to have a doctor write a letter to this effect**.

ESA's are allowed to fly as well and live in housing that would otherwise say "No Animals."

However, under the current ACAA and FHA (Air Carrier Access Act and Fair Housing Act) an

ESA is only protected as follows:

An ESA may fly in the cabin of a commercial or private airline with their handler, and the handler does not have to pay a pet or other fee. A very specific prescription letter from a licensed mental health profession is typically ALWAYS required by airlines, as well as advance notice in most cases that the passenger will be flying with an ESA.

Landlords and property managers must make reasonable accommodations for tenants or prospective tenants with ESAs, even if the apartment, house, college dorm, or other residence does not allow pets. Reasonable fees may be asked of the client, similar to a pet fee. Besides requiring a letter of prescription. Property managers/landlords may require that the (prospective) tenant's mental health professional complete and sign a Third Party Verification form.

Service animals are defined as dogs that are **individually trained to do work or perform tasks for people with disabilities.** Examples of such work or tasks include guiding people who are blind, alerting people who are deaf, pulling a wheelchair, alerting and protecting a person who is having a seizure, reminding a person with mental illness to take prescribed medications, calming a person with Post Traumatic Stress Disorder (PTSD) during an anxiety attack, or performing other duties. Service animals are working animals, not pets. **The work or task a dog has been trained to provide must be directly related to the person's disability.** *Dogs whose sole function is to provide comfort or emotional support do not qualify as service animals under the ADA.* If you have an emotional support animal please visit our website at **esaregistration.org.**"

March 22, 2016

Unknown bird, but it does go underwater every now and again

Collette squinting, bright day

A large turtle and an anhinga

March 21, 2016

An anhinga thoroughly enjoying the first day of spring.

Calm and cool.

It definitely likes throwing its fish around

and playing with it before it gulps it down.

03.20.2016

Tiniest turtle I have seen thus far on this body of water.

My Sweet Collette

Interesting video on treating cancer with immunotherapy:

http://www.discovercarebelieve.org/discover-our-breakthroughs/pd-1/#

"12 ways meditations can solve more problems than you realize" whisper / Lifestyle (March 19th 2016 5 am article)

1) Sometimes, you just need to look within yourself to find the confidence you need

2) There's nothing like being at peace with yourself to make you more at peace with others

3) There's no more magic to negative energy than there is to positive energy--so spread that positivity!

4) When it's working for you, meditation will make you realize you don't need a substance to feel good

5) Once you find a healthy outlet to fulfill you, it's good to implement it into your life more permanently

6) Although it's good to find contentedness through a healthy practice, you shouldn't solely rely on it for happiness

7) The best outlets may come to you in ways you'd never expect

8) <u>Self-control</u> can help you through so many negative

9) There's no better feeling than getting back into a practice you once loved

10) You <u>can heal yourself</u> through meditation in even the most difficult of struggles

11) Get to know yourself better so you can <u>forgive yourself</u> for the things plaguing you

12) It's funny when you realize that things that once felt so big are actually so small

<u>By the way highly recommend:</u>

 via youtube.com – **"self-hypnosis: Become a relationship magnet" – Collin Rosati**

"Discover the power of prosperity" (dvd) **by Rich Guzzi** (the comedian and hypnotist) or check out some funny clips on youtube.com in reference to his hypnosis comedy show.

March 19, 2016

Newest set of ducklings

03 18 2016

Collette at doggy daycare.

Lolly and Collette down below.

Thank you, V.I.P!!!

March 18, 2016

March 18, 2016

My Certifications/Licenses:

Pilates - alignment of the body, toe correctors, better posture, range of motion = better sense of overall health - otherwise you will end up hunched over and not walking in a balanced manner, particularly in your elder years.

"Physical fitness system developed in the early 20th century by Joseph Pilates (from Germany). He referred to it as, "contrology". He believed if it was practiced with consistency, pilates improves flexibility, builds strength and develops control and endurance int he entire body. It puts emphasis on alignment, breathing, developing a strong core, and improving coordination and balance."

- from wikipedia.org

Esthetician/Facial Specialist - "Skin is the largest organ of the human body" SPF of 30 plus = highly beneficial from the rays of the sun. maintaining cleanly, moisturized skin = overall healthier mode of being. Be aware of what is in your skin products, otherwise can cause an adverse reaction when combined.

Reiki - (otherwise pronounced Ray-kee) - "A Japanese technique for stress reduction and relaxation that also promotes healing. IT is administered by "laying on hands" and is based on the idea that an unseen "life force energy" flows through us and is what causes us to be alive. If one's "life force energy" (also known as qi (pronounced, chi) is low, then we are more likely to get sick or feel stress, and if it is high, we are more capable of being happy and healthy." **- by Reiki.org**

Developed by a Japanese Buddhist, Mikao Usui (1922).

- by wikipedia.org

Life Coach - "A person who counsels or motivates others in the achievement of personal objectives such as choosing or changing careers, improving relationships, setting goals, and determining priorities"

 - from thefreedictionary.com

ABC Bartending School **-** It was interesting to learn but it is probably more beneficial to learn in an actual bar. The main component they don't teach you is the overall exhange of drinks/money and dealing with stereotypical customers (their behaviors).

Permanent Make-up Specialist - definitely go to <u>a board certified class</u>, I instead went to an individual. I wasted mucho dinero on something that was not very legit in my mind...hence why I never followed through with it. Hard earned money down the drain.

Eye Lash Extension Specialist - It was interesting to learn but definitely choose a class with more than just yourself. Also, more than just a few hours/a day. Practice makes perfect especially for such a tedious process.

Bachelor's Degree:

Communications - learning body language, nonverbal/verbal. Interactions between individuals and reading between the lines. Helpful in learning human behavior patterns.

Public Relations (minor) - learning about case studies of Public Relations going horribly wrong was insightful. Crisis management.

Prior Job Experiences include:

(food prep, bus girl, waitress, newspaper sales, swim shop attendant, front desk - graveyard shift, government "intern", matchmaker, promotions personnel, well known babysitting referral service employee, w.c. model, customer service personnel, hotel front desk staff member, independent contractor, cosmetics company seller, etc...)

All of this equates to character building, meaning that having ethics ("ethos") is essential. Being responsible, timely and accountable. Catering to the customer, listening and understanding how to communicate effectively are important components.

March 17, 2016

(one of my oldest poems, but still my #1 favorite)

The Sun Will Rise
With or Without You

Each day the sun will rise,

every spring the flowers will bloom,

the birds will sing their cries,

and one day I will be

with whom?

Each day the sun will rise,

the grass will grow,

no one ever wants to hear goodbyes,

a black bird will crow.

Each day the sun will rise,

I won't be here forever,

while the roaring ocean sighs,

<u>and you just might not be clever</u>,

to know these things will happen,

with or **without** you.

March 17, 2016

Collette, pretty in pink

Odd black birds

March 17, 2016

Amazon.com

March 17, 2016

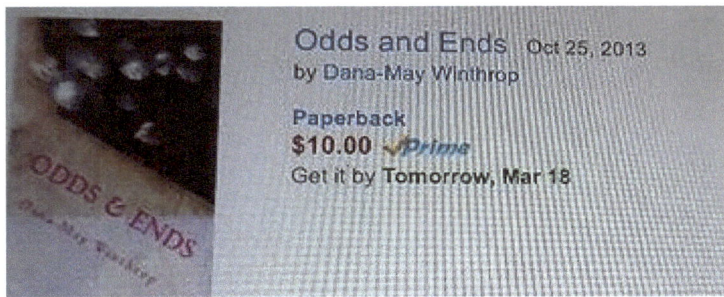

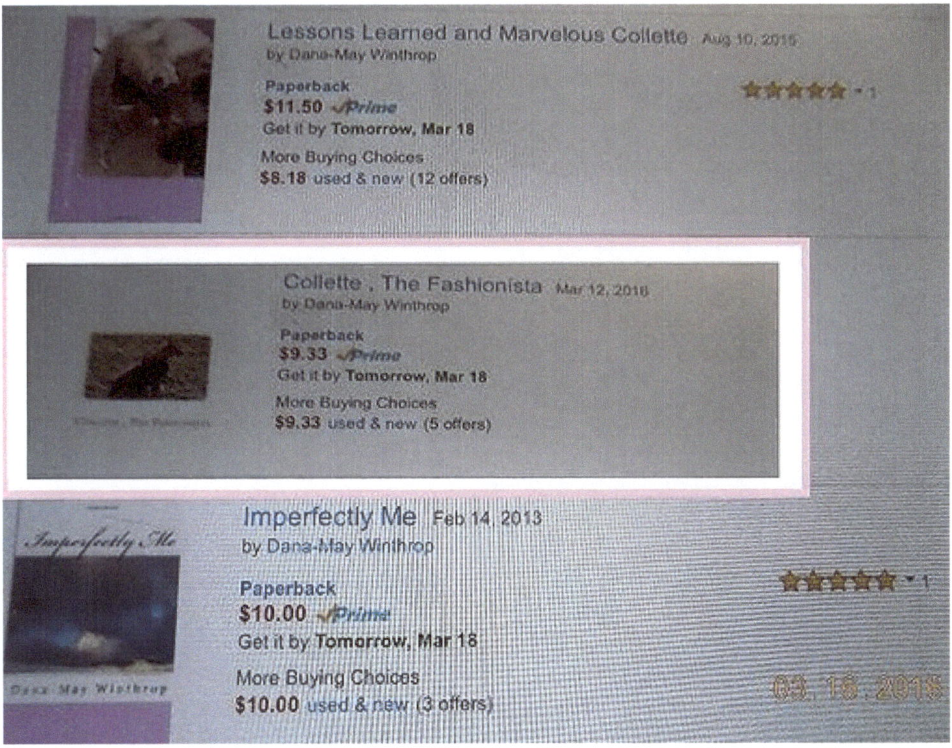

Odds and Ends Oct 25, 2013
by Dana-May Winthrop

Paperback
$10.00 ✓Prime
Get it by **Tomorrow, Mar 18**

Lessons Learned and Marvelous Collette Aug 10, 2015
by Dana-May Winthrop
Paperback
$11.50 ✓Prime
Get it by **Tomorrow, Mar 18**
More Buying Choices
$8.18 used & new (12 offers)

★★★★★ ▾ 1

Collette , The Fashionista Mar 12, 2016
by Dana-May Winthrop
Paperback
$9.33 ✓Prime
Get it by **Tomorrow, Mar 18**
More Buying Choices
$9.33 used & new (5 offers)

Imperfectly Me Feb 14, 2013
by Dana-May Winthrop
Paperback
$10.00 ✓Prime
Get it by **Tomorrow, Mar 18**
More Buying Choices
$10.00 used & new (3 offers)

★★★★★ ▾ 1

03.18.2016

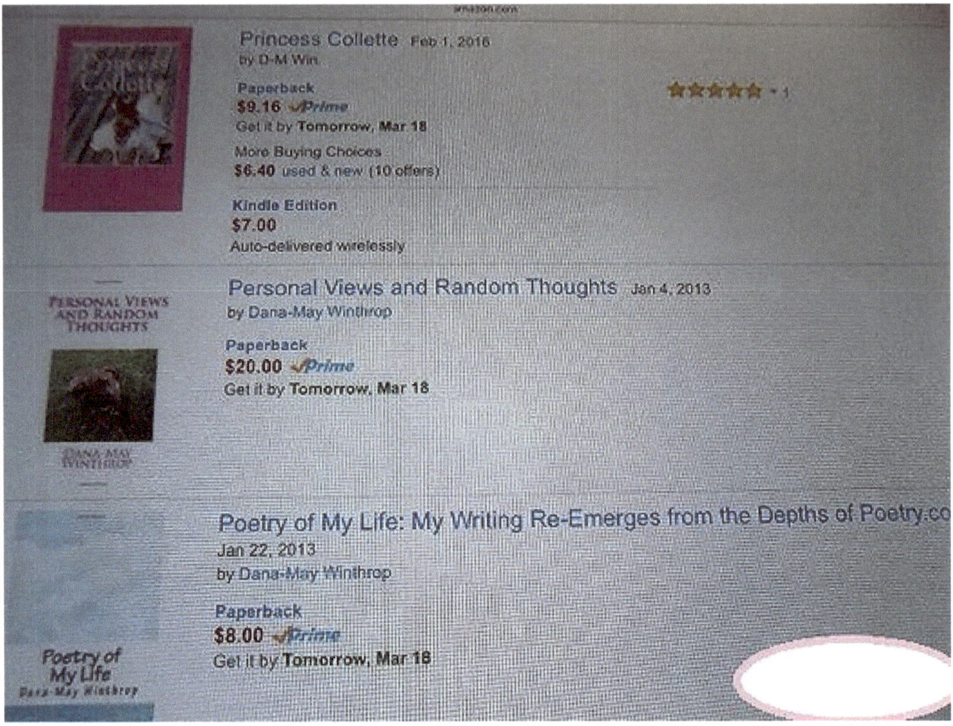

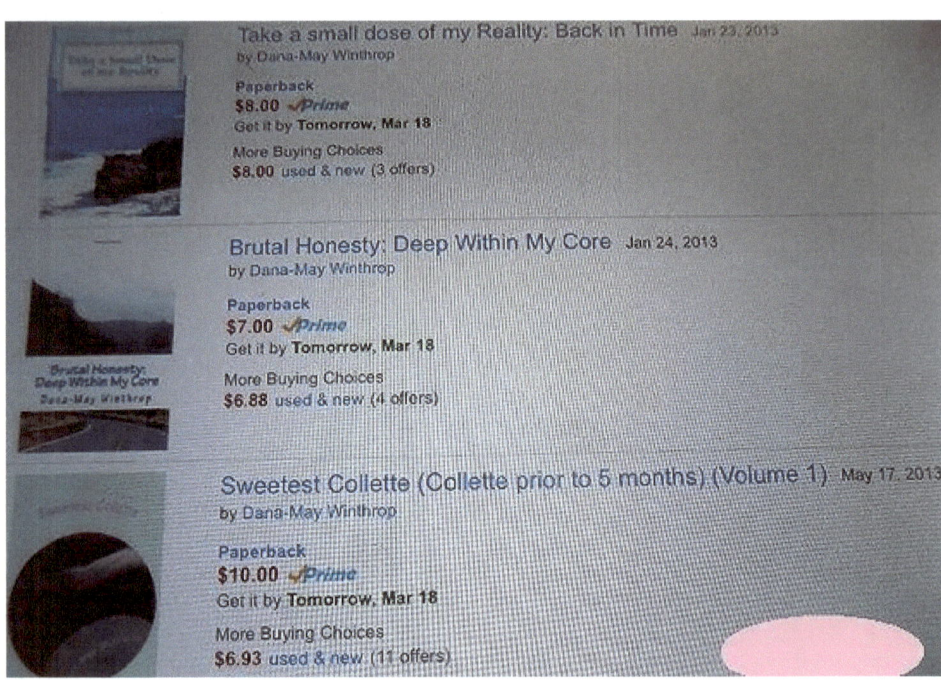

Princess Collette Feb 1, 2016
by D-M Win

Paperback
$9.16 *Prime*
Get it by Tomorrow, Mar 18

★★★★★ ▾ 1

More Buying Choices
$6.40 used & new (10 offers)

Kindle Edition
$7.00
Auto-delivered wirelessly

Personal Views and Random Thoughts Jan 4, 2013
by Dana-May Winthrop

Paperback
$20.00 *Prime*
Get it by Tomorrow, Mar 18

Poetry of My Life: My Writing Re-Emerges from the Depths of Poetry.co
Jan 22, 2013
by Dana-May Winthrop

Paperback
$8.00 *Prime*
Get it by Tomorrow, Mar 18

Take a small dose of my Reality: Back in Time Jan 23, 2013
by Dana-May Winthrop

Paperback
$8.00 *Prime*
Get it by Tomorrow, Mar 18

More Buying Choices
$8.00 used & new (3 offers)

Brutal Honesty: Deep Within My Core Jan 24, 2013
by Dana-May Winthrop

Paperback
$7.00 *Prime*
Get it by Tomorrow, Mar 18

More Buying Choices
$6.88 used & new (4 offers)

Sweetest Collette (Collette prior to 5 months) (Volume 1) May 17, 2013
by Dana-May Winthrop

Paperback
$10.00 *Prime*
Get it by Tomorrow, Mar 18

More Buying Choices
$6.93 used & new (11 offers)

March 17, 2016

March 16, 2016

Today's pictures, always amusing...

03. 16. 2016

http://danamaywin05.wix.com/mysite

CODESTER

COLLETTE

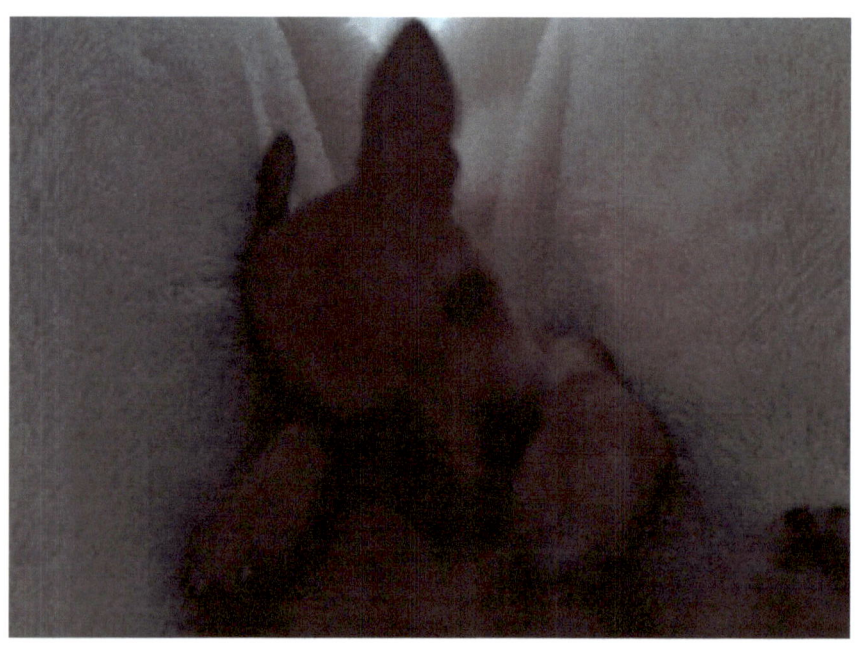

HAWAII

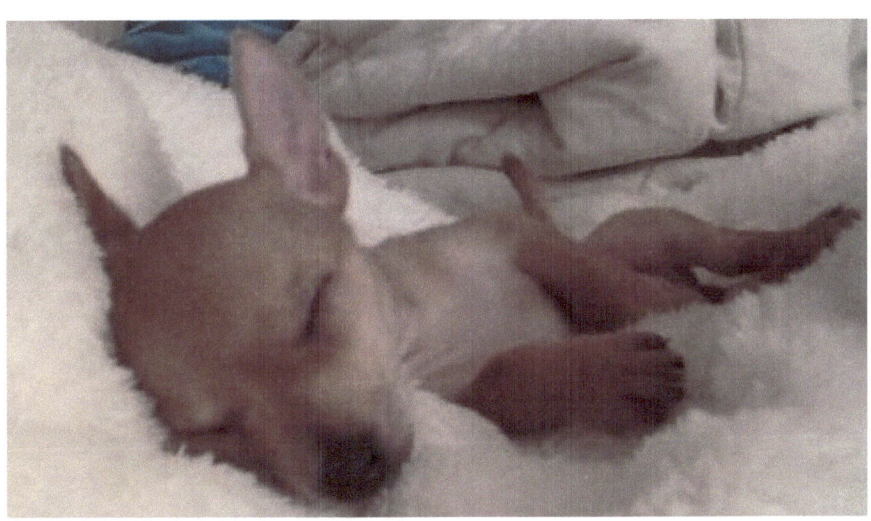

ALL PICTURES TAKEN BY:

DANA-MAY WINTHROP

Except those taken by V.I.P (doggy daycare)

Life is a conundrum, **make the most of it**.

Collette is my darling pup who brightens my day.

<u>To inspire and bring about positive changes</u>, isn't that our sole purpose for being here?

More than anything, thank you to my supporters and *most of all THANK YOU to my family and friends*. You keep me grounded.

March 9, 2016

There is something majorly wrong with our society when such cases as a puppy's head gets smashed by an individual's foot or a person physically cutting a women's womb open - to steal their unborn baby or when a person's physical facade is ruined forevermore because of acid being thrown in his/her face...these things justifiably **should equal a punishment that is just as severe as what those demented individual's have done** which is to physically harm/injure a living being with unjustifiably *violent means.*

Death Chamber, for those individuals, don't even bother wasting the American people's hard earned money for *a jail system where they get free room and board, free healthcare, food, and a means of learning, growing and reproducing.* **Is that fair?**

Killing a person/animal should automatically be like Monopoly - GO DIRECTLY TO JAIL. NO FREE GET OUT OF JAIL CARD, EVER.

I pray that rapists who are known for *repeat offenses* or those who *continually commit crimes* are **punished and extinguished**.

People who live in the real world and are law abiding citizens should not have to constantly fear for their lives due to the lack of our judicial government ruling harshly to those who "have reaped what they have sowed".

Certain things in history, should not have to be repeated. **If only we learn to do better.**

March 9, 2016

When I think of Ben Higgins (from the Bachelor), it oddly reminds me of, "My Fair Lady" which is one of my all-time favorite musicals. I think this season resonates with most women who watch it, is because it gives single women, **hope**. Hope that such a guy like Ben, who is *honest, sincere and invested in finding true love*, does actually exist. Even Chris Harrison, the host compliments him.

Either way, it is nice to see.

POLITICS

Ok, so on another - entirely opposite topic. One is never supposed to discuss politics but...some things just need to be said, especially if it is important enough. Let's boil it down...

Trump - so far he has demonstrated that he does indeed discriminate, speaks his mind without a filter, will say anything and do anything that will help his ratings, really is fueled by hate/anger. Does he really sound like a good candidate who is supposed to empower the American people? Perhaps he should stick to being a television villain, in his next job position. (Important tidbit, what Romney stated about Trump's work history background)

Hilary Clinton - the same old, same old. Who stands by their man, when he consistently cheated...and the lying bit is becoming old news.

Will the Real Presidential Candidate, please stand up?

I am still waiting for the real contenders to come to the forefront.

March 5, 2016

TV SHOWS

Eli Stone

The Guardian

Dead Like Me

MOVIE

Spare Parts

SONG

" Save Me" by TiMO ODV

WEBSITE

teamtreehouse.com

March 5, 2016

There is no use arguing with someone who already has made up his/her mind. (But clearly, I definitely jinxed myself from my prior posting...)

Greatest Admirable Trait

what I admire most

are those people

who take you in

as their own

who never question your motivations

for why you do the things you do

and instead takes you

for who you are

and gives so much of themselves

it is the greatest admireable trait

of humanity

Who will be the one?

Crazy tragedies have been

occurring in our nation

why war continues on

in this day and age

no one really knows

prejudice surrounds us

suffocates us

until we are unable to breathe

lies grow rampant all around the world

for what purpose does it continue to exist

But to destroy the ones we love

hatred lives on

revenge

sweet bitter revenge lies deep within our hearts

a slight change of uncertainty can unleash

all of the mishaps of Pandora's box

who will be the bravest of the brave

who will be the courageous one to show the world by example

what it is we are supposed to be fighting for

A just and worthy cause

not this mentality of an eye for an eye

surely not stooping to the same level or lower

than those who are acting out their anger

Who will be the one?

<u>Did you know?</u>

Did you know

that person who you knocked down

one too many times

was an angel in disguise

did you know she was a martyr

a heroine of sorts

she will reign again

but did you know

you were the one

who hated her so

and yet she continued on

and loved

and shared of dreams so true

were you not

the one who disgraced her so?

IRONY

IT IS IRONIC

HOW ONE CAN INITIATE A CONVERSATION ONLINE

MADLY ONE CAN FALL IN LOVE

WHAT MAKES AND BREAKS

THIS SORT OF RELATIONSHIP

IS WHEN YOU ACTUALLY

HAVE TO MEET THAT SOMEONE

WHO YOU HAVE DECLARED YOU LOVE

WITH ALL THE DEVOTION ONE CAN MUSTER

THE SPLIT SECOND YOU MEET

A GROAN ESCAPES YOUR LIPS

AND YOU WANT TO RUN

BUT INSTEAD YOU HAVE TO WAIT IT OUT

AND FORCE YOURSELF

TO BE POLITE

AND ACT AS THOUGH YOU HAVE CARED ALL ALONG

WHEN IN ACTUALITY

THERE IS NO CHEMISTRY

BETWEEN YOU AND YOUR ONLINE LOVER

HOW TERRIBLY TRAGIC

AND YET

WELCOME TO THE 21ST CENTURY

A wink and a nod

The price of beauty is often severe

people nowadays get lazured

to vanguish those wrinkles

they get punctured by doctors

to take out their fat

people often do

the most strangest of things

some people get new noses

while others starve themselves

how absurd that

people like your uncle, your aunt

or even your mom and dad

do these ridiculous things

the price of beauty

is a miraculous thing

after all

by the way did I tell you

I had all of these done?

CRAZY TO MARRY

IN THIS DAY AND AGE

I WONDER HOW EVEN A 21 YEAR OLD

COULD GET MARRIED

HAVEN'T YOU HEARD THE NEWS

OF PEOPLE OF EVERY AGE

SPLITTING UP OR DIVORCING?

DON'T YOU KNOW THE STATITICS INVOLVED?

HAVEN'T YOU BEEN LISTENING?

I'M NOT A PESSIMIST BY ANY MEANS

BUT OPEN UP YOUR EYES

I WORRY THAT YOU'LL SOON LEARN OF YOUR FATE

A BIT TOO LATE

DON'T RUSH INTO THINGS

THAT YOU WILL LATER REGRET

I AM LOOKING IN YOUR BEST INTEREST

FOR I AM ASTOUNDED IF I WERE TO WED

AT SUCH AN AGE

MY AGE

I CAN'T FATHOM IT

NOR IMAGINE A WORSE FATE

YOU HAVE SO MUCH TO DO

DON'T GET TIED DOWN

HEROES IN OUR MIDST

THANK YOU TO OUR DEARLY UNNAMED HEROES

THOSE WHO DO NOT SEEK OUT

FAME, MONEY OR GLORY

INSTEAD THEY WALK AMONGST US

MAKING SURE WE ARE SAFE AND SOUND

THEY ARE OUR NEIGHBORS

WHO ARE MERELY STRANGERS IN OUR EYES

THEY ARE POLICEMEN, FIREMEN, GOVERNMENT
OFFICIALS, TEACHERS, SOLDIERS

OUR COUNTRYMEN

THOSE STRANGERS WHO WILL STOP AND HELP A POOR
FELLOW ON THE ROAD

THOSE PEOPLE WHO CARE FOR ANOTHER STRANGER

AS THOUGH THEY ARE THEIR OWN

THANK YOU!

Unbeknownst to him

Not long ago

I too loved a "prince"

he rode in gallantly

in his shining armor

I, too was smitten

by his heroic tales

and believed in all his glory

it is he

I still dream about

It is he

who unknowingly crushed my heart

shattered it into a million pieces

it was he

who showed the least bit of care

for he strode out

out of my life

and never did he look back

www.ingramcontent.com/pod-product-compliance
Lightning Source LLC
Chambersburg PA
CBHW050810290526
45792CB00001B/64